PRAY
FIERCE

I0459754

For Your Marriage

A JOURNEY OF HEALING AND RESTORATION THROUGH PRAYER

LETICIA SEMBERA

FIERCE
PUBLISHERS

Copyright © 2025 Leticia Sembera

All rights reserved. No part of this publication may be reproduced, distributed, or transmitted in any form or by any means, including photocopying, recording, or other electronic or mechanical methods, without the prior written permission of the publisher.

ISBN 978-1-962775-04-5 (Paperback)
ISBN 978-1-962775-06-9 (Hard Cover)
ISBN 978-1-962775-05-2 (eBook)

Scripture quotations marked "NIV" are taken from the Holy Bible, New International Version®, NIV® Copyright © 1973, 1978, 1984 by Biblica, Inc.™ Used by permission of Zondervan. All rights reserved worldwide.

Scripture quotations marked "NLT" are taken from the Holy Bible, New Living Translation, copyright © 1996, 2004, 2007 by Tyndale House Foundation. Used by permission of Tyndale House Publishers, Inc., Carol Stream, Illinois 60188. All rights reserved.

Scripture quotations marked "NASB" are taken from the New American Standard Bible®, Copyright © 1960, 1962, 1963, 1968, 1971, 1972, 1973, 1975, 1977, 1995 by The Lockman Foundation. Used by permission.

Scripture quotations marked "NKJV" are taken from the New King James Version. Copyright © 1982 by Thomas Nelson, Inc. Used by permission. All rights reserved.

Published by Fierce Publishers

First printed 2025

To my husband, you have always been and will always be the love of my life — thank you for allowing me to share this.

Those who sow in tears shall reap in joy.

Psalm 126:5 (NKJV)

Table of Contents

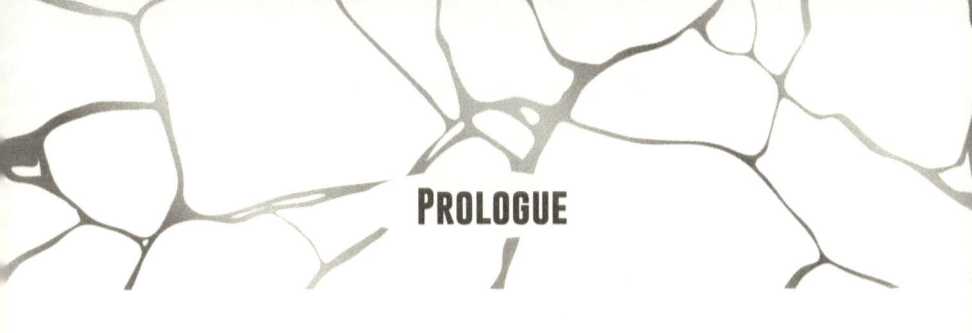

The Beginning

My husband and I met in 1993, when I was 18 and he was 24. We had both had kids (boys) early in life and had both recently broken up with our prior partners. When I broke up with my boyfriend, I was living in an efficiency apartment with my roommate. Both of us had grown up in church and neither of us knew how to dance, so we were looking for someone to show us. I had another friend who would always talk about what a good dancer her brother-in-law was so she offered to introduce us.

When he walked in the room, the energy changed (it still does). He was funny, in a corny kind of way, and just fun, something I needed after being in a toxic relationship. We started dating and after only three months, he went away for a "state paid vacation." I had just started college and promised to write, but honestly told him if I met someone else, I was not going to stop for a boyfriend that was "in the pen" (18-year-old me was hysterical).

In total honesty, when we had talked about the future, I always knew I would want to "go back to church" and live a life like how I had grown up. I had a baby (who was 2 at the time) and I wanted to give him the same sort of childhood I had. He had told me he was not interested in going to church all the time but he was not opposed to going *sometimes*. As soon as he said that, I figured he was not the one for me and I truthfully did not ever intend to stay together with him.

To my surprise, he got saved "in there" and gave his life to Jesus. Instead of the girl who grew up in church leading him to the Lord, it was the other way around. He encouraged me to find a church and start going again – so I did.

When he got home, we visited all the churches that visited

AUGUST 1997

him. After three years of basically a pen pal type relationship, we were finally able to be together. Because I had been in an abusive relationship before, I was waiting for the time when this one would get bad. I kept counting the months, then the years for when things would start "falling apart" but they never did. I loved him and he loved me.

We were opposite in so many ways but we complemented each other well. I love to cook and he loves to clean. I like to plan and he is happy to go with the flow. I am an introvert and he is definitely an extrovert. While I am studying strategies on how to lower taxes or different types of financial investments, he is studying how to juggle four balls or different

HE LETS GO, EYES OPEN! I HOLD ON, EYES CLOSED --- APRIL 2017.

ways to mount a unicycle. I do kids ministry; he does prison ministry. I get excited when I discover a new restaurant, he gets excited when he learns a new coin or card trick. I help him set goals and think about the future; he helps me laugh and not take myself too seriously. We balance each other.

Now, we have reached the point where we have been together longer than we have ever been apart. We have so many "first time" memories together because we truly grew up together.

However, we did not keep God in the center of our marriage and it eventually took its toll. A marriage is just like a garden. You cannot plant something and never water it, never pull weeds, and expect it to be beautiful and thriving. Eventually, weeds (distractions) start crowding the pretty flowers and you need to pull them – we did not. Eventually, the ground that

3

was once healthy and strong will need watering (intentional dating) – we did not. And little by little, decision by decision, we ended up in a place neither of us wanted.

But God!

God changed everything. God's word renewed my mind. He restored our marriage. He made everything brand new. Before I shared all these prayers from during this difficult time, I just wanted you to know a little bit about our story.

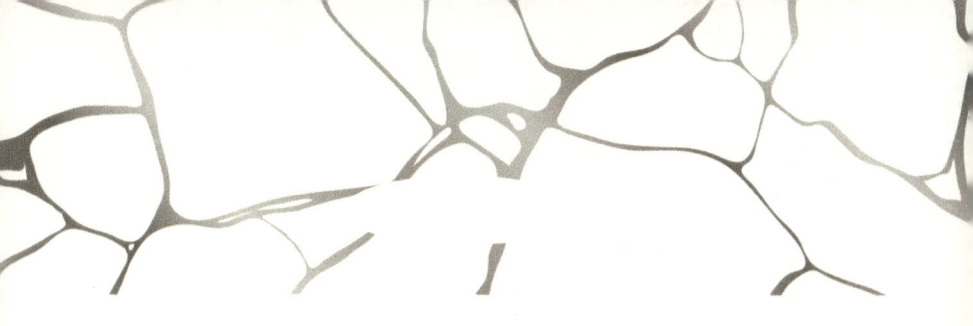

Introduction

Time elapsed: 1 year, 2 months

I am writing this introduction exactly 1 year and 2 months – to the day that I wrote my first prayer. Wow! Until I looked at the date just now, I did not realize this. If I compare where I am now, to where I was then, it feels like a lifetime ago. God has done a quick work and I am truly amazed!

As I was thinking through subtitles for the book, I went through many. Most people did not know what happened or why I wrote the book, so this title was like my first time telling everyone. It was the first time revealing a very personal and fragile thing about our marriage. At first, I just wanted it to be plain and clear – like when you rip a bandaid off all of a sudden - Pray Fierce for your Marriage – the prayers I wrote after the affair. Or, the prayers that renewed my mind after the affair. Or, prayers that restored my mind and heart after betrayal. But because most people did not know what had even happened, it felt too shocking. I kept imagining my kids reading it or their friends. And even though they all knew, it was hard to see it in print like that. For my first book (<u>Pray</u>

Fierce) when I was looking for help with a subtitle, I surveyed my Facebook group and asked people to vote. This time, I did not feel comfortable doing that. With the help of two friends, I settled on what it is – A Journey of Healing and Restoration through Prayer. And it's perfect because that is just this is. This is my personal story. These are prayers that I wrote during a very dark time in my life, yet through it all – God was there.

GROUND RULES

Before I start, I wanted to clear up some things and set some expectations.

1. **This is <u>not</u> a tell all book** where all the disgusting details of all that has happened gets spilled. The details are not important. This book is about the healing process. It is about what happened *after*. It is about how the word of God (that is alive and active) went to battle with every crazy thought I had in my head. This book is about how I used God's Word to renew my mind and show that you can, too.

2. **I am not a therapist**. I am not pretending to be. I am sharing how *I* used the word of God to pull me out of something dark. By sharing these deeply personal prayers, my hope is to support someone who might be navigating the same struggles I once faced and provide a practical example of how you can use the word of God to renew your mind.

3. **I am <u>not</u> going to villainize my husband**. The truth is that we both stepped out on our marriage at different times. (Yes, you read that right.) We *both* broke our commitments to each other. The difference is that this time, I was rooted and grounded in the word so I fought *differently*. I healed completely and restoration happened. You see, the enemy operates in secrets (in the dark), but we know that we overcome by the blood of the Lamb and by the word of our testimony (Rev 12:11). So, while it was hard to share all this in a book and make it public – I knew I *had* to.

4. **I am not promising you will have the same results**. But I do want you to know that God is NO respecter of persons (Acts 10:34) – this means He does not have favorites, what He does for one, He can do for all. There is nothing special about me, I just had faith that God would do what He said. I had faith that He could and would restore my marriage and He did. I believe if you have that same faith – He **can** and *will* do the same for you – but it is up to *you* to believe.

5. **We both had to put in real work**. There were things we both needed to work on within ourselves and as a couple. We were both open to that. It was not an overnight restoration, but it was a restoration nonetheless.

You have no idea how many times I went back and forth about whether I should publish this or not. It is not easy to put your life out there for display. I kept thinking if I say it, it's out there and there is no way to take it back. Once I publish it, there is no way to go back to a time when no one knew. But I could not shake the feeling that I needed to do this. I knew in my spirit that I was supposed to.

After discussion with my husband and kids, I knew I had to. Even though it's hard, I think we all understood that we always should consider God's purpose over our preference. Still, I went back and forth so many times and each time I wanted to back out, I would get a confirmation to move forward. That is how I knew. He kept gently pushing me forward. 2 Corinthians 1:4 (NLT) says, "He comforts us in all our troubles so that we can comfort others. When they are troubled, we will be able to give them the same comfort God has given us." I pray this book will bring comfort and healing to you.

CHAPTER 1

Punch to the Throat

When I first found out what happened, I was devastated. I was angry, hurt, sad. Nothing can really prepare you for that punch in the throat. And the enemy starts right away to begin replaying conversations in your mind. The hypotheses start forming about missing timelines *"that's where he must have been that day when…."* *"No wonder he was late that one time when…"*

Things got very messy for a while. The kids found out. We separated for a short period. Everything came out of the dark. And I mean everything – everything I did way back when and everything he did. The kids found out *everything.* I was so sad and very embarrassed. And though it hurt so much at the time, I know now that everything had to be exposed because the enemy works in the darkness – but he cannot handle the light.

We both decided that we wanted to make it work but obviously it was difficult for me to trust again.

I knew that I needed to write some prayers. I needed to remind myself of what the word of God said about what I was feeling.

I had done this before with my first book (Pray Fierce). It had helped me so much to write prayers when I was feeling emotions like sad or ashamed or confused. It helped me to know what God's word said about my situation and then pray according to *that* instead of continuing to feed my feelings. I was a newer believer then. But now, I was more spiritually mature and I felt in my spirit that I needed to do the same thing again. I knew that it would help because the word of God is the only thing that can battle those thoughts planted by the enemy and renew the mind. But at the time, I could not. I even remember saying out loud, *"I know I need to write them God, but I cannot right now. I promise I will."* God is so gentle. Even as I write this, I feel a warm embrace.

I wrote the first prayer about a month and two weeks after I found out. From that point on, any time I started feeling some kind of way, I just wrote my thoughts, even if they were not complete sentences. Even if it was just phrases, I wrote down what I was thinking and then I wrote a prayer to combat every thought that did not align with the word of God. I realize now what I was doing – I was renewing my mind with the word of God.

When I was done, I had 10 prayers. I did not plan it like this, it just happened. What I also did not plan is that they would each cover a specific topic, like The Past or Not Feeling Good Enough. Each topic is represented as a chapter in this book.

Each chapter is formatted very similarly:

written font

This section at the very beginning of every chapter is where I document the thoughts I wrote back then and the elapsed time that had passed from the day I first found out. I did not edit these very much because I wanted to leave the exact words that I wrote at that time. It was like a little diary to God.

PRAY THIS

This section is prayer that I wrote at the time when I had the thoughts. The verses referenced in the prayer are also included. Take these prayers and pray them. Modify them for your situation. The prayers of the righteous are powerful and effective! (James 5:16 NIV)

SAY THIS

This section has powerful statements to declare out loud about yourself and your situation. **Do not skip this** – there is a very strong connection between what we believe and what we say out loud. It is not only Biblical but psychological. Speak these declarations over your life boldly and with confidence even if it does not seem like reality. Remember, we call things that are not as though they are (Romans 4:17 KJV).

If you are reading this, I am assuming either you or someone you know may be going through a difficult situation in your marriage. For me, it was betrayal, but for you, maybe it is a different situation. Regardless, the word of God can help renew and restore anything that has been broken. Maybe you are at week one or month one or even year two of your own journey. Whatever the case, I hope you realize that God loves you, that you are made with a purpose and that none of whatever has happened cancels any of that out.

God can restore. And when God restores, He not only "fixes," He makes brand new. He makes *new* creations. He makes things BETTER. But restoration starts first with you. *Your* mind must be renewed. *Your* thoughts need to be transformed. What God has said about you has to be so ingrained in your mind that you do not have room for anything else. This is what God did for me. And if He did that for me, He can and *will* do it for you. Your job is to have faith. What does it mean to have faith? It just means to trust that God is not a liar. It means to trust God will keep His word.

I know your thoughts may be going crazy right now -- *What if he/she does not change? What if it happens again? What if I cannot forgive? What if?* – I am going to ask that you do not try to figure any of this out right now. Isaiah 26:3 (NKJV) says, "You will keep him in perfect peace, whose mind is stayed on You, because he trusts in You." Do not worry about what will happen next. Do not keep playing the *What If* sound track. Just keep your mind on Him, and you will stay in perfect peace.

I also realize that for some of you, a reconciliation may not be possible. Maybe your former spouse is remarried or unwilling or fill-in-the-blank. Again, that is ok. This book is focused on renewing <u>your</u> mind. Feel free to modify any prayer and any affirmation to <u>your</u> situation. The Word of God always works. Before any new relationship starts, your mind must be renewed and ready.

CHAPTER 2

The Unsolved Puzzle
MOVE FORWARD

Time elapsed: 6 weeks after

I keep googling, searching trying to find new things. It is like I cannot leave it alone. I keep trying to piece this puzzle together and maybe I am not supposed to finish it. Maybe I am not supposed to see how it was. I had not wanted to write these prayers because it is too painful but I need to. We are called to comfort others with the pain we receive.

Those were the first words I wrote when I finally decided to write my prayers. Six weeks had passed since I had found out. After a brief separation, my husband and I were committed to working on our relationship - but everything was a mess at home. There was a lot of hurt and trust issues.

One of the hardest things for me was simply moving forward. I wanted to figure out every aspect of what happened. *Where? How? Why? Is that where you were when...?* I wanted to have every question answered, but the answers did not really help like I thought they would, they just brought more pain. I wanted to know, but the more I knew, the more it hurt.

I had to stop torturing myself with this and force myself to find scriptures in the Bible that dealt with the past. I know what I wanted to do, but what did the Bible say to do? The Bible says in Philippians 3:15 to "forget what is behind and strain towards what is ahead." You cannot move forward if you do not stop looking backward. I am not saying do not deal with the problems or implement safeguards in your relationship, I am saying do not wallow in the past. You **cannot** move forward this way.

The Bible very clearly states that we are to forgive others just like He has forgiven us. There is no stipulation that the person you are forgiving must "be repentant." I know that may be tough to hear, but that is between *them* and God. You need to forgive because God has forgiven *you*.

I knew that I had also done things I was very ashamed of and God had forgiven me and transformed me. Just as I was forgiven, I needed to forgive. I could not do this on my own, I needed divine help for this. I knew I was a changed person and that I could never do any of the bad things I had done in my past because I loved and feared the Lord too much. I could never do that again because the Lord's been too good to me and I understood that I would be doing it to Him. If God had caused me to understand this, I knew He could also do that same work in my husband. I had to forgive.

I heard a story in a message a couple of years ago that has always stayed with me. The speaker said scientists had conducted an experiment and put a locked cage in the middle of a rainforest. Inside the cage was a bunch of bananas. The bananas could not fit through the bars.

During the experiment, something fascinating happened. Monkeys would reach into the cage to grab a banana and get caught because they would not let go. Picture that. The cage was not a trap. The monkey could have dropped the banana at any time and freed its hand from within the cage but instead chose to hang on to its prize. It seemed tragic to me. Tragic that these monkeys would choose to remain trapped because they would not let go of something.

But that is exactly what we do when we do not let go of the past. We stay stuck in a place where we were never meant to stay. Let go. Let God fix it. (Forgiveness does not make them right, it makes you free.)

PRAY THIS

Heavenly Father,

I come to you in the mighty name of Jesus, thanking you for one more day. Thank you for forgiving me. Thank you so much for forgetting my past.[1]

Lord, help me move forward. Help me look in front of me and to stop reliving the past. Just like you have forgiven me, help me to forgive.[2] Help me to keep moving forward pressing forward to what lies ahead not what is behind.[3]

Love is patient and kind. Love does not keep a record of wrongs. Love forgives all. Love does not lose hope. Love does not end. Love is a choice.[4]

Help me to love when I do not feel like it. Help me be more like you.[5]

In Jesus' Name,

Amen

THE VERSES REFERENCED

1. **Isaiah 43:25** (NIV) "I, even I, am he who blots out your transgressions, for my own sake, and remembers your sins no more.

2. **Colossians 3:13** (NIV) Bear with each other and forgive one another if any of you has a grievance against someone. Forgive as the Lord forgave you.

3. **Philippians 3:13-14** (NIV) Brothers and sisters, I do not consider myself yet to have taken hold of it. But one thing I do: Forgetting what is behind and straining toward what

is ahead, I press on toward the goal to win the prize for which God has called me heavenward in Christ Jesus.

4. **1 Corinthians 13:4-7** (NIV) Love is patient, love is kind. It does not envy, it does not boast, it is not proud. It does not dishonor others, it is not self-seeking, it is not easily angered, it keeps no record of wrongs. Love does not delight in evil but rejoices with the truth. It always protects, always trusts, always hopes, always perseveres.

5. **John 3:30** (NIV) He must become greater; I must become less."

SAY THIS

I declare in the name of Jesus that:

- I confidently look forward to the new thing God is doing in me and for my family.
- I know God is working to perfect everything which concerns me.
- My best days are before me and not behind me because I go from glory to glory, victory to victory and strength to strength.
- I wholeheartedly love and forgive others just like God loves and forgives me.
- I rest easy knowing God has a plan for my life and a future to prosper me.

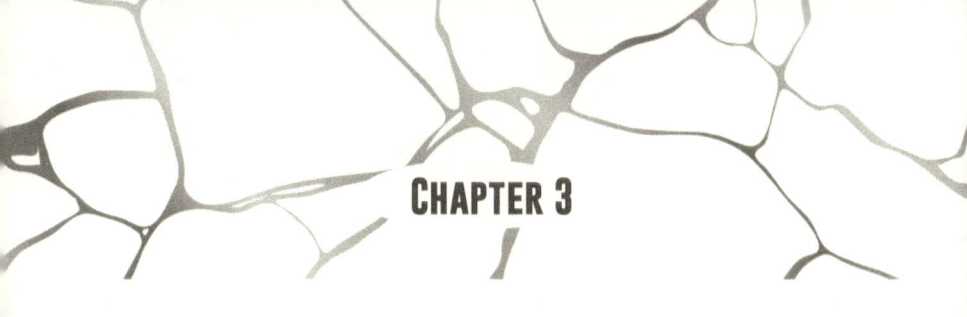

CHAPTER 3

Why?

DEALING WITH ALL THE QUESTIONS

Time elapsed: 8 weeks after

My heart is broken in a million little pieces. And those pieces feel broken in a million more. My heart physically hurts and I am so tired of obsessing over this. I am tired of thinking about this over and over. I feel like I am grasping at straws...does he love me or does he feel trapped? I guess that is what I keep thinking about. And that one thought sort of opens the floodgate of questions...

Does he want to be with me or is he with me because it is easier? Is that the only reason he is here? Does he think about her when he is with me? Does he love her?

I wrestle with these questions on and on until I am in tears. I do this multiple times a day.

One of the things that I struggled with was trying to understand <u>why</u>. *Why did this happen? What did I do?* I could not sit in "quietness" because my mind was constantly at war with all these thoughts swirling around. Did I ever get a solid reason why? Meh. I do not know. Even if I would have gotten some "reason" why it happened, the bottom line is that it was wrong. It should have never happened. Even if I was acting some crazy way against my spouse would that ever provide justification for an affair? No. One wrong does not justify another wrong.

For example, let us say I was a horrible person – that I was mean and neglectful and not a good wife. Would that give my husband a "valid" reason to have an affair? No, it would not. No matter how I acted, he would <u>never</u> have justification to have an affair. You see, one wrong, does not justify another wrong. Does him having an affair now give *me* a justification to act horribly towards him? Also no. Because, one wrong does not justify another wrong.

For any relationship to work, there is some self-evaluation that must happen on both sides. The self-evaluation must happen not against how the other acts, but how the Word of God instructs us to act.

What I finally came to realize is that I can only change myself. I cannot change my husband or anyone else. I am also not the Holy Spirit; I cannot convict anyone. I cannot keep guilt-tripping people to make them feel a certain way. At some point, I stopped wondering why he did it and started asking myself if I had been acting the way I should have been.

I started to examine and evaluate *myself* next to what the Word of God says. The Bible states in 2 Corinthians 13:5 (NLT) "Examine yourselves to see if your faith is genuine. Test yourselves." Am I being a good wife? Are my words encouraging? Am I uplifting with my words? Am I practicing Biblical love? Am I being kind? Am I being the best wife I can be? When I really sat down and did this, I realized there were things I needed to work on.

Was he doing all this? I mean, was he evaluating himself? I do not know. Sometimes, it did not feel like it. But, again, one wrong does not justify another wrong. I got the revelation that I am not responsible for *his* actions, I am only responsible for mine. I will not have to answer for *his* actions, I will only answer for mine. I know that when I meet Jesus face to face, I want to hear "well done good and faithful servant."

My goal in life is that I want to do everything as if I am doing it for the Lord. Everything. In all areas – and that includes my marriage.

Did I eventually get all questions answered? No. Will I ever? Probably not. In truth, nothing he could ever say would ever really be enough – so there is no point. But, the more I lived my life according to what the Word of God said, the less it mattered. I want to be in right standing because I want to please my Father above all. I also realized that once my husband truly understood the revelation I had—that he alone would be accountable for his actions—he would strive to become the best husband he could be. Not just for my sake, but because he would genuinely desire to honor God by giving his very best.

Do not stay stuck trying to figure out why. Just lay those questions down and begin to examine yourself against the word.

PRAY THIS

Heavenly Father,

Lord, I come to you in the mighty name of Jesus thanking you for watching over me.

I cannot take this never-ending doubt. I cannot think about this anymore. I am taking all these unanswered questions and laying them at your feet. I am laying them all down one by one at your feet.[1]

I surrender it all. It is all yours. I will press forward; I will forget the past.[2] I will remember that Love does not keep a record of wrongs. Love chooses to love at all times. [3] I will do my part so you can do yours.

I give all the questions to you. I capture every thought and force them to think about you. [4] I will keep my mind on you so that you can keep me in perfect peace. [5]

In Jesus Name,

Amen.

THE VERSES REFERENCED

1. **Matthew 11:28** (NIV) "Come to me, all you who are weary and burdened, and I will give you rest.

2. **Isaiah 43:18** (NIV) "Forget the former things; do not dwell on the past.

3. **1 Corinthians 13:4-7** (NIV) Love is patient, love is kind. It does not envy, it does not boast, it is not proud. It does not dishonor others, it is not self-seeking, it is not easily angered, it keeps no record of wrongs. Love does not delight in evil but rejoices with the truth. It always protects, always trusts, always hopes, always perseveres.

4. **2 Corinthians 10:5** (NIV) We demolish arguments and every pretension that sets itself up against the knowledge of God, and we take captive every thought to make it obedient to Christ.

5. **Isaiah 26:3** (NIV) You will keep in perfect peace those whose minds are steadfast, because they trust in you.

SAY THIS

I declare in the name of Jesus that:

- I am in perfect peace because I trust God's plan for my life and I keep my mind on Him.
- God's perfect love has cast out any fear I had.
- God is restoring all the time that was stolen from me.
- I embrace every new season God has for me.
- I expect goodness and kindness to follow me all the days of my life.

CHAPTER 4

Not Enough

DEALING WITH NOT FEELING GOOD ENOUGH

Time elapsed: 3 Months after

The thing that I have been thinking about is that I am not enough. I keep replaying things said and trying to understand why. Why? Then the comparison games begin. Anything that he does that is even slightly different than normal gets questioned because maybe that is what he did with her. At the core I keep agonizing over this ==> What did she have that I did not have? Why was I not enough?

My self-esteem took a beating. I had always looked in the mirror and basically liked what I saw. I am not saying that I didn't have things I could work on, I am just saying, I was not nitpicking my faults. I had never felt old or ugly. But after this, I began to magnify every flaw that I saw in the mirror. I started counting those wrinkles and gray hairs. I started to notice the wrinkles around my eyes. Those extra pounds seemed to laugh at me every time I looked in the mirror.

But I thank God for His word to remind me that my identity does not come from any man. As I began to write this prayer, I began to remind myself that I am made in God's image. I am a precious gift. I am made for His special purpose. I am a royal priesthood! I am the daughter of the King! And as the King's daughter I refuse to walk around with my head hung low.

Every time I felt like this, I would pray this prayer. I would meditate on these scriptures. I would reject every lie the enemy tried to place in my mind and replace it with the Word of God.

You are more than enough. You are made for a special purpose. You are a royal priesthood. You are the daughter/son of the King! And as the daughter/son of the King, you will not walk around with your head hung low.

PRAY THIS

Heavenly Father,

Thank you. Thank you so much for these private counseling lessons. Thank you for letting me come to you and pour my heart out.

My identity comes from you. You say that I am perfectly made in your image.[1] I am a precious gift. I am made for a special purpose[2]. I am a one-of-a-kind design. I am part of a royal priesthood[3], a citizen of heaven[4]. I am yours. You chose me[5]. You, the God of all creation, chose me!

I will reject any lie that the enemy tries to put in my head that does not align with your word. I will remember who I am in Christ. And I will run to you, my strong tower[6] when I feel sad or afraid or like I am not enough.

Thank you for your promises for my life. Thank you for holding my future in your hands[7].

In Jesus name,

Amen

THE VERSES REFERENCED

1. **Genesis 1:27** (NIV) So God created mankind in his own image, in the image of God he created them; male and female he created them.

2. **Ephesians 4:1b** (NIV) "...I urge you to live a life worthy of the calling you have received."

3. **1 Peter 2:9** (NIV) But you are a chosen people, a royal priesthood, a holy nation, God's special possession, that

you may declare the praises of him who called you out of darkness into his wonderful light.

4. **Philippians 3:20** (NLT) But we are citizens of heaven, where the Lord Jesus Christ lives. And we are eagerly waiting for him to return as our Savior.

5. **John 15:16** (NLT) You didn't choose me. I chose you. I appointed you to go and produce lasting fruit, so that the Father will give you whatever you ask for, using my name.

6. **Proverbs 18:10** (NKJV) The name of the LORD is a strong tower; The righteous run to it and are safe.

7. **Jeremiah 29:11** (NIV) For I know the plans I have for you," declares the LORD, "plans to prosper you and not to harm you, plans to give you hope and a future.

SAY THIS

In the name of Jesus, I declare:

- I am a one-of-a-kind masterpiece, no one else is like me.
- I am made in God's image and I am beautiful inside and out.
- I know that overwhelming victory is mine!
- The favor of God makes me stand out everywhere I go.

- I am always joyful and genuinely happy because I know I am never alone.
- I confidently walk with my head held high because I am the daughter/son of a King!

CHAPTER 5

Twisting Words
LEARNING HOW TO EXTEND GRACE

Time elapsed: 3 Months after

I keep twisting his words. I know I am doing it. I keep having suspicious thoughts so anything he says is suspect and if I am not in His Word, I use it as an excuse to begin a hostile conversation. It is like I am looking to start a fight, but I do not want to fight. He is not good with words. I know that. Why am I not extending grace? I would do it for anyone else.

Let us pretend someone says to you "*wow, you look soooo nice today.*" Most people would respond with a quick thank you or a smile. But imagine if you said something like "*why do you look surprised? what are you trying to say? I usually look horrible?*" You know that is not what they meant, but either as a joke or for whatever reason, you choose to put words in their mouth that they did not say and it makes the conversation take an awkward turn. *THIS* is what I was doing.

As an example, I would maybe ask him if he wanted to go out for a walk and he may say no, he is tired and I would respond with something like "*of course, you are always tired for me but never too tired for other people.*" It was like he was walking egg shells around me because I could and would explode at any moment for something he did not say or imply – I just wanted to fight. And, I also know my husband is not good with words. He is not the kind of person that can string together a beautifully crafted sentence or apology. He has never been like that. Normally, I give him grace in this area because his actions normally speak louder than his words. But, during this time, I kept picking apart and dissecting every sentence. I was very critical and watchful of every word. I cannot explain why I did this, but I know it must have been the enemy just wanting to keep me in turmoil.

Make no mistake, it is the enemy that comes to steal, kill and destroy. He wants to destroy your marriage, destroy your relationship, destroy your trust, destroy your peace of mind. But it is up to us to not allow that to continue. It is hard to just move on from something like this, but I kept saying to myself that I have the mind of Christ. My goal is to be more like Him. I refuse to use my own words to tear down anyone, period.

PRAY THIS

Heavenly Father,

Thank you for loving me no matter what. Thank you so much for your unconditional love.

Lord, I am so sorry. I am so sorry that I keep using my words to hurt someone else[1]. It is not about what they did, it is about what I am doing with my own tongue. Please help me to use my words to encourage and uplift[2]. Help me say kind words that uplift not tear down. I know the power of life and death is in the tongue[3]. Please help me not use my own words to tear and kill my relationship[4].

I love you. Thank you so much for changing me, for removing my sin nature[5], for forgiving me[6].

In Jesus name I pray,

Amen

THE VERSES REFERENCED

1. **Colossians 4:6** (NIV) Let your conversation be always full of grace, seasoned with salt, so that you may know how to answer everyone.

2. **1 Thessalonians 5:11** (NIV) Therefore encourage one another and build each other up, just as in fact you are doing.

3. **Proverbs 18:21** (NKJV) Death and life *are* in the power of the tongue, And those who love it will eat its fruit.

4. **Proverbs 6:2** (NIV) you have been trapped by what you said, ensnared by the words of your mouth.

5. **Romans 8:9** (NLT) But you are not controlled by your sinful nature. You are controlled by the Spirit if you have the Spirit of God living in you. (And remember that those who do not have the Spirit of Christ living in them do not belong to him at all.)

6. **1 John 1:9** (NIV) If we confess our sins, he is faithful and just and will forgive us our sins and purify us from all unrighteousness.

SAY THIS

In the name of Jesus, I declare:

- I have the mind of Christ, totally renewed, and refreshed.
- I daily encourage and uplift others.
- I am led by the spirit and speak according to His word.
- I give grace to others easily and willingly.

CHAPTER 6

Investigative Reporter
DEALING WITH ALL THE SUSPICIOUS THOUGHTS

Time elapsed: 3 Months + 5 days after

I am not a jealous person. I do not have a jealous nature. I do not investigate and dig and question, because my nature is to trust, to believe. But suddenly, I am checking phone records. I am checking location; I am checking friends' lists. I do not want to do this. We are in a content place where everything is good and I know we are going to make it and then the enemy will pop a thought in my mind and I can feel myself go down a rabbit hole of investigation. I do not want to keep doing this. At the end of the day, I must trust. I must give God the room to do work in him.

Three months had passed and things had settled into a new norm. I do not want to say things were "all good," but things were better - at least they seemed to be on the surface. But inside, I was constantly brewing, constantly scheming. The reason I know it was the enemy planting thoughts is because everything would literally be fine and suddenly, as I am watching tv or sweeping, I would have a random thought and then I would start searching and digging. I honestly do not know what I was looking for, I was just looking.

If you are doing this, I want you to know that you cannot live like this. At some point (I am not saying three months is the point, I am just saying at some point), you must begin to rebuild trust. You cannot be wondering if something is going on 24/7.

This is also not something that can be done alone. My husband was really trying. We had worked together to develop new boundaries. He was not being unfaithful. We had changed churches during this time and he rededicated his life to Christ. His life had taken on a new trajectory. He was so on fire for things of the Lord and I *knew* he was not doing anything with anyone. The enemy was just trying to keep my mind in turmoil.

I decided that I could only change me. I wanted to love like God wanted me to love. I wanted to be a good wife, regardless of whether I felt like he deserved it or not. I knew that God was working on my husband and I decided I would not ruin that with my words of distrust. I knew that God was going to be my defender. He would not allow me to be put to shame. I hung on to these promises and focused on changing within and letting God change my husband.

Not all the thoughts in your mind come from God. Identify the ones that do not align with God's word and purge them. Make up your mind that the enemy will **not** use your mind as his personal playground.

PRAY THIS

Heavenly Father,

I come to you today in the name of Jesus thanking you for giving me the mind of Christ[1]. I thank you for transforming me on the inside.

Lord, I want to follow you with my whole heart. I want to be like you want me to be. I want to love like you want me to love[2]. Love does not keep a record of wrongs. Love assumes the best, hopes for the best. Love endures all things[3]. I am trying to love like this. Please help me. I do not need to be distrustful because I know you are just. You see all and you will not allow me to be put to shame[4]. You will expose what is hidden[5] and you will protect me[6] and my heart. Even when it does not feel like any real change is happening in my husband, I will put my trust in you because I know are always working on my behalf[7,8].

Thank you for the peace that I can rest in. Flood my thoughts with thoughts of you.

In Jesus name I pray,

Amen

THE VERSES REFERENCED

1. **1 Corinthians 2:16 (**NLT) For, "Who can know the LORD's thoughts? Who knows enough to teach him?" But we understand these things, for we have the mind of Christ.

2. **John 13:34** (NIV) "A new command I give you: Love one another. As I have loved you, so you must love one another."

3. **1 Corinthians 13:4-**7 (NIV) Love is patient, love is kind. It does not envy, it does not boast, it is not proud. It does not dishonor others, it is not self-seeking, it is not easily angered, it keeps no record of wrongs. Love does not delight in evil but rejoices with the truth. It always protects, always trusts, always hopes, always perseveres.

4. **Psalm 25:3a** (NIV) No one who hopes in you will ever be put to shame

5. **Luke 8:17** (NIV) For there is nothing hidden that will not be disclosed, and nothing concealed that will not be known or brought out into the open.

6. **Psalm 121:3** (NIV)The LORD will keep you from all harm— he will watch over your life;

7. **2 Corinthians 5:7** (NKJV) For we walk by faith, not by sight.

8. **Exodus 14:14** (NIV) The LORD will fight for you; you need only to be still."

SAY THIS

In the name of Jesus, I declare:

- I have the mind of Christ, totally renewed, and refreshed.
- I love others wholeheartedly like God has loved me.
- I am patient and kind and do not keep a record of wrongs.
- I trust others because I know the Lord will never allow me to be put to shame.
- My mind is always at peace because God daily fights for me.

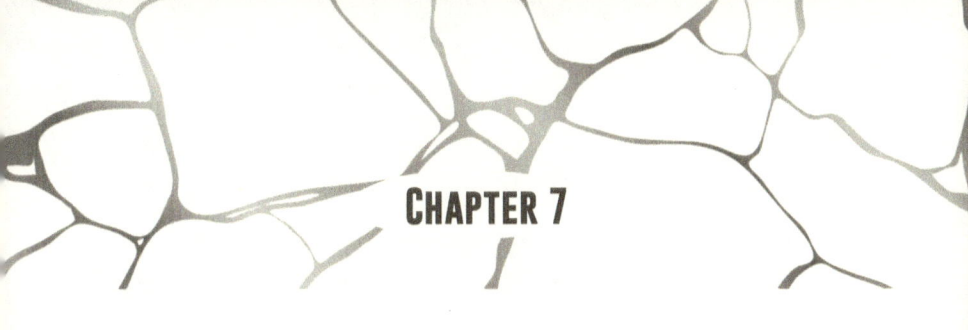

CHAPTER 7

Jesus Lens

LEARNING TO SEE OTHERS LIKE JESUS DOES

Time elapsed: 3 months + 5 days after

Part of me wishes I did not know so much. I hate knowing what she looked like, how old she was, what she did for a living. And although I hate to admit this, I find myself looking at other women who look similar or who I think he may be attracted to and I see them through this lens. I see them through my lens of being hurt and I can feel myself being jealous, suspicious. I do not want to be like this! Part of my ministry is to help women. How can I help them when I am suspicious of them if they look a certain way? I am so sad about this. I do not want to be like this.

I remember one day I was walking out of a department store. I was pushing my cart to the car and that is when I noticed the lady in front of me. She was a very pretty lady, probably about ten years younger than me. She was dressed very casually with leggings and a t-shirt and I remember looking at her and thinking how pretty she was and then suddenly, a thought came into my mind out of nowhere – *I am glad my husband is not with me, this is probably somebody he would be attracted to.*

I think as soon as I had that thought, I was a little bit shocked. Those are not my usual thoughts. I do not think like this. Almost just as instantly I felt a conviction and ever so gently, I felt like God told me, *"How can I use you to minister to women if you see them through this lens?"* I remember crying about this realization. It broke my heart to think that God would not be able to trust me in this area. I kept thinking, *"What if she needed help? What if God had a message I needed to deliver? He will never trust me to do this if I feel this way."*

As I mentioned at the beginning of the book, I wrote these thoughts and prayers initially when I first found out, but I am writing this "middle" part of the journey of healing almost two years later. As I read these thoughts again, it both breaks my heart to remember how I felt then, but also makes me feel joy and relief because I do not feel like this anymore – at all. I am not sure when I stopped having these feelings, I just know I do not have them anymore.

If you are experiencing thoughts that keep you rooted in the past, loving past the pain may be tough initially, but remember that we are to love others as God loves us. We need to see people through a Jesus lens, not through the lens of our own pain. You cannot do this on your own. But, with Jesus, you can do all things.

PRAY THIS

Heavenly Father,

Thank you, Lord, for the privilege to call myself a Christian. Thank you for loving me and for forgiving me of all my sins. Thank you for sending your only son to die for my sins[1] when I did not deserve it[2].

I want to see people like *you* see them[3]. I want to love my neighbor just like your word says[4] I should. I want you to use me. I do not want to see a certain kind of person and start imagining things that are not aligned with your word. Lord, let me remember during those times that I have the mind of Christ[5]. I can take all those thoughts captive and force them to obey[6]. Help me remember that your word says to pray for *all* people[7]… not just those I want to pray for. Let my burden for those who are lost be greater than any other emotion I feel.

I know you can change all things[8]. I know that you will hear my plea and help me. Thank you for being available.

In Jesus name, Amen

THE VERSES REFERENCED

1. **John 3:16** (NIV) For God so loved the world that he gave his one and only Son, that whoever believes in him shall not perish but have eternal life.

2. **Romans 5:8** (NASB) But God demonstrates His own love toward us, in that while we were still sinners, Christ died for us.

3. **John 13:34** (NIV) (Jesus speaking) "A new command I give you: Love one another. As I have loved you, so you must love one another."

4. **Matthew 22:39** (NIV) And the second is like it: 'Love your neighbor as yourself.'

5. **1 Corinthians 2:16 (**NLT) For, "Who can know the LORD's thoughts? Who knows enough to teach him?" But we understand these things, for we have the mind of Christ.

6. **2 Corinthians 10:5** (NIV) We demolish arguments and every pretension that sets itself up against the knowledge of God, and we take captive every thought to make it obedient to Christ.

7. **1 Timothy 2:1** (NLT) I urge you, first of all, to pray for all people. Ask God to help them; intercede on their behalf, and give thanks for them.

8. **Mark 10:27** (NIV) Jesus looked at them and said, "With man this is impossible, but not with God; all things are possible with God."

SAY THIS

In the name of Jesus, I declare:

- I have the mind of Christ, totally renewed, and refreshed.
- I think God-like thoughts of everyone I encounter.
- I see others through the eyes of Christ and love wholeheartedly like God has loved me.
- I daily pray for others and intercede on their behalf.
- I can easily comfort others with the same comfort I have received from the Lord.

CHAPTER 8

Not Wanted

WHEN YOU FEEL TOTALLY UNLOVED

Time elapsed: 3 months + 2 weeks after

It is very sad to feel not wanted. I feel like he thinks he is doing me a favor by staying here and I want to scream sometimes at the top of my lungs to JUST GO. I DON'T CARE. It sometimes feels like he is angry at me because I ended his very fun affair. Like if it wasn't because of me, his life would still be fun but because of me it is boring.

I met my husband when I was 18. I had just broken up with my first baby daddy (haha) and I remember being very sad. I was living with a roommate at the time and both of us had grown up in church so neither of us had ever been to a club or knew how to dance. We were looking for someone to teach us how to dance and another friend of mine offered to introduce me to her brother-in-law, who was a great dancer. I had heard her complain about him multiple times because he was always trying to get his brother (her boyfriend) to go out when they argued. But she insisted he was a great dancer, so my roommate and I met him because he was going to teach us both to dance. We went to see Selena for our first date at a local club. And we just sort of clicked. He walked into the room and "lit things up." You either really liked him or could not stand him, but there was no in between.

We had one of those relationships where we were always together. He is the great love of my life. We enjoyed being together. Someone once told me that my eyes would light up any time I spoke about my husband and I know it is because I genuinely adored him. Please do not misunderstand that to think we never had issues or problems; I am not saying that. What I am saying is that I genuinely loved him and I had always felt like he genuinely loved me.

But after all this happened, I didn't feel that anymore. I felt like he resented me -- like he was being forced to be with me, even though he *chose* to come back. He *wanted* to stay. I felt like he did not want to be there. If I am being honest, I do not know if what I was feeling was real at the time, or if I was imagining it but I was always "looking for authenticity" in everything he did and was extremely suspicious. More than anything, I did not want to feel like a charity case.

I want you to know that no matter what happens, even if you feel like no one loves you, God loves you. God made you as you are and you are beautiful in His eyes. You are made in His image and your identity comes from Him. He has a wonderful plan for your life. He has a wonderful future planned for you. The word of God says that you will go from glory to *glory* and strength to *strength* and victory to *victory*. This means your life will get *better and better*, <u>not</u> worse. Your best days are in <u>front</u> of you, not behind you. You are loved more than you know.

PRAY THIS

Heavenly Father,

Thank you for my life. Thank you for my family and my marriage. Thank you for every good and perfect gift you have given me[1].

I will block out every word that does not align to your word[2]. I will hold every thought captive that does not align with your word[3]. My identity does not come from man. It comes from you. Your word says that what YOU have put together, let no man separate[4]. I will make room for what you want to do because I know that you are perfecting everything concerning me[5].

Lord let me hear your words louder than I hear anyone else's words.

In Jesus name I pray,

Amen

THE VERSES REFERENCED

1. **James 1:17** (NIV) Every good and perfect gift is from above, coming down from the Father of the heavenly lights, who does not change like shifting shadows.

2. **Proverbs 30:5** (NLT) Every word of God proves true. He is a shield to all who come to him for protection.

3. **2 Corinthians 10:5** (NIV) We demolish arguments and every pretension that sets itself up against the knowledge of God, and we take captive every thought to make it obedient to Christ.

4. **Mark 10:9** (NASB) Therefore, what God has joined together, no person is to separate."

5. **Psalm 138:8** (NKJV) The LORD will perfect that which concerns me; Your mercy, O LORD, endures forever; Do not forsake the works of Your hands.

SAY THIS

In the name of Jesus, I declare:

- I have the mind of Christ, totally renewed, and refreshed.

- God has planned a wonderful future for me and my family.
- I am beautiful, fit, and strong.
- I can handle any challenge with grace because I do not fight alone.
- My life keeps getting better and better.
- More and better opportunities keep coming my way.
- God is perfecting everything concerning me.

CHAPTER 9

Incoming Thought
DEALING WITH ALL THE RANDOM THOUGHTS

Time elapsed: 3 months + 2 weeks after

Things are going great and suddenly; a weird thought will pop in my mind. A random thought that came from nowhere. It sends me spinning again. Where did he go last Tuesday when he was gone for a while? Is he on FB again? Then in an instant, my peace is gone and the private investigator in me comes out and starts digging and digging. What am I looking for? I do not even know.

I wrote this thought/prayer the same day that I wrote the previous chapter (Not Wanted). It is interesting that I start this off by saying *"things are going great and suddenly…"*, when earlier in the day I must have felt unwanted and wrote the previous prayer. I only point this out because its evidence that I was in a mental rollercoaster for a while. All these prayers and scriptures were helping to renew my mind, but it was still a process. I kept letting the devil use my mind as a playground. I would entertain every destructive thought.

I heard this example that really made sense to me. The speaker was explaining that thoughts are coming in and out of your mind every day like people in a hotel lobby. Imagine that thoughts are coming in and out of a rotating door like people come in and out of a hotel lobby. Not all thoughts in your mind come from God. The enemy plants thoughts in your head too. And some of these thoughts are destructive, belittling, suspicious. You need to be able to identify those thoughts and push them out of your mind with the Word of God as quickly as possible just as if you were pushing them out of the hotel lobby door. Instead of pushing those thoughts out the door, I was checking those thoughts in a room. Then visiting the thought. Then having dinner with the thought. Instead of immediately rejecting it, I had invited them to stay as a long-term guest. The enemy was using my mind as a playground and no doubt laughing as I kept riding this emotional rollercoaster.

Do not do this. As soon as you recognize a thought that does not align with the Word of God, CANCEL IT OUT WITH HIS WORD. Example, a thought comes in your mind "*how will I ever make it?*" – Easy, you will make it because you can do all things through Christ (Philippians 4:13). Another thought, "*I do not want to live my life alone.*" -- you will not, because He will never leave you or forsake you. You are never alone (Deuteronomy 31:6). Another thought, "*how will I ever trust my spouse again?*" – you will because God is a restorer of things. He will restore you (Psalm 71:20). He will not let you be put to shame (Psalm 25:3).

As you continue to resist the thoughts, the enemy *has* to flee – its scriptural (James 4:7). This is how you renew your mind. This is how you take every thought captive. **Fight those thoughts back with the Word.** Let God's Word get so deeply ingrained in your mind that those thoughts do not stand a chance.

PRAY THIS

Heavenly Father,

Thank you for every single promise in your word. Thank you for loving me and sending your only son to die for me[1].

I know if I stay focused on you, you will keep me in perfect peace[2]…so help me stay focused on you. I take every thought captive[3] and force it to think about you. Help me stay focused on you and your promises. I am not the Holy Spirit, I cannot convict. Help me stay focused on you and let me make room for you to do your perfect work in my husband and in me. Love trusts. Love is hopeful and endures through every circumstance[4]. Help me love the way you command it in your word. Help me love him the way you love me[5].

In Jesus name I pray, Amen.

THE VERSES REFERENCED

1. **John 3:16** (NIV) For God so loved the world that he gave his one and only Son, that whoever believes in him shall not perish but have eternal life.

2. **Isaiah 26:3** (NLT) You will keep in perfect peace all who trust in you, all whose thoughts are fixed on you!

3. **2 Corinthians 10:5** (NIV) We demolish arguments and every pretension that sets itself up against the knowledge of God, and we take captive every thought to make it obedient to Christ.

4. **1 Corinthians 13:4-**7 (NIV) Love is patient, love is kind. It does not envy, it does not boast, it is not proud. It does not dishonor others, it is not self-seeking, it is not easily angered, it keeps no record of wrongs. Love does not delight in evil but rejoices with the truth. It always protects, always trusts, always hopes, always perseveres.

5. **John 13:34** (NIV) (Jesus speaking) "A new command I give you: Love one another. As I have loved you, so you must love one another."

SAY THIS

In the name of Jesus, I declare:

- God is moving mightily in my life and changing circumstances around.
- I am capable of loving others just like God loves me.
- My mind is at peace because it is daily focused on the Lord.
- My mind is renewed and restored.
- There is nothing I cannot do if I remain in Christ.
- I have new strength given to me daily that is enough to face any challenge.

CHAPTER 10

Kintsugi Type of Relationship
RENEWING YOUR MIND TAKES WORK

Time elapsed: 6 months + 9 days after

Everything is going better. A new "better" normal is happening. God has truly transformed my husband; I can visibly see it. But sometimes, I start feeling myself being suspicious, doubting, overthinking. Is he only going to church because he wants to see someone there? I am not a jealous person so why do I keep having these thoughts? I do not want to feel like this. I do not want to think like this. These are not my thoughts. Lord, please help me.

One day as I was on my way to pick up my son from school, I had a supernatural experience. I had been feeling sad, heavy, like I was sinking. The Bible says for the spirit of heaviness, put on a garment of praise. So, on the way to pick up my son, I forced myself to put some music on and worship. You see, sometimes you must do things even if you do not feel like it. Your feelings will catch up. I put on one of my favorite upbeat songs called "I'm Blessed." Some of the words – *"I'm the head and not the tail, above and not beneath, I'm an overcomer and I walk in victory…where the Spirit of the Lord is there is liberty…and the spirit of the Lord is inside of me…I'm blessed."* (I am forcing myself to stop, because all the lyrics are good. If you have not heard it go listen!) Anyway, I played this song loud. I sang it out loud. I did not feel like doing this, but I did it anyway. I played it non-stop as I drove and after a little bit, and I began to feel joy.

As I was driving and singing, I remembered something. I had recently told someone that when words are said, it is like a plate that is broken and glued back together – it can never be the same. I was saying this as an example of how hurt I was. I was remembering our prior love and mourning the fact that it would never be exactly like that again. But then God reminded me about the Japanese art form of Kintsugi. In Kintsugi, they take a broken plate and they "glue" it back together with gold. It takes an ordinary item and makes it extraordinary. It takes an ordinary plate and makes it priceless and unique.

In that moment, in the car, I felt like God was telling me…" *you are right, things are broken now and they will never be the same – but just like Kintsugi…things can be better. Much, much better."* I remember so clearly even now, years later. I cried then and I am crying now as I write this because God is so good. He had heard me and I knew He was doing a work in my husband and in me and in our marriage.

The renewing of your mind can take time, but it is time well spent. Fight back every thought with the Word of God. Give a sacrifice of praise even when you do not feel like it. You are priceless! Anything can be restored! And when things are restored by God – they are not the same – they are better! Much, much better.

Pray This

Heavenly Father,

I come to you today in the mighty name of Jesus. Thank you for restoring my marriage. Thank you for changing my heart.

Lord, help me. I feel so ashamed for having these thoughts. I want to trust wholly. Show me how.

When I am feeling like this remind me that the enemy comes to steal, to kill and to destroy[1]. I will rest on your word and your word alone[2]. You are doing a new thing[3] and I will not ruin it with my words[4]. I will not allow the enemy, the author of confusion[4], to plant thoughts that do not align with your words.

Lord, I take every thought that does not align with your word and cast it out[6]. I have the mind of Christ[7]. I am renewed[8]. I have been redeemed[9]. My marriage has been restored.

In Jesus mighty name,

Amen.

THE VERSES REFERENCED

1. **John 10:10** (NIV) The thief comes only to steal and kill and destroy; I have come that they may have life, and have it to the full.

2. **Proverbs 3:5** (NKJV) Trust in the LORD with all your heart, And lean not on your own understanding;

3. **Isaiah 43:19** (NIV) See, I am doing a new thing! Now it springs up; do you not perceive it? I am making a way in the wilderness and streams in the wasteland.

4. **Proverbs 6:2** (NIV) you have been trapped by what you said, ensnared by the words of your mouth.

5. **1 Corinthians 14:33** (NKJV) For God is not *the author* of confusion but of peace, as in all the churches of the saints.

6. **2 Corinthians 10:5** (NIV) We demolish arguments and every pretension that sets itself up against the knowledge of God, and we take captive every thought to make it obedient to Christ.

7. **1 Corinthians 2:16 (**NLT) For, "Who can know the LORD's thoughts? Who knows enough to teach him?" But we understand these things, for we have the mind of Christ.

8. **2 Corinthians 5:17** (NKJV) Therefore, if anyone *is* in Christ, *he is* a new creation; old things have passed away; behold, all things have become new.

9. **Isaiah 44:22** (NKJV) I have blotted out, like a thick cloud, your transgressions, And like a cloud, your sins. Return to Me, for I have redeemed you."

SAY THIS

In the name of Jesus, I declare:

- My relationship is better than it has ever been.
- I use my words to encourage and uplift others.
- I fully love others the way God loves me.
- I am beautiful, strong, and confident.
- My life keeps getting better because I go from glory to glory and strength to strength.
- My mind is fully at peace because I know God fights for me.

CHAPTER 11

Almost There

THANKING GOD FOR A DIVINE RESTORATION

Time elapsed: 10 months after

Many months have now passed. At the beginning of the year, my pastor prayed for me and said that I would struggle to remember any of this. And this is what I would like to pray for as well. It feels like I am almost there, but sometimes, out of nowhere, I will remember something. I keep replaying, start googling again, almost making sure I do not forget. But no, I will not keep doing this to myself. The past is gone. He is a new man. I have forgiven. No more.

During this year, many things changed in our day-to-day life. This took work. You cannot assume that restoration happens and you will not have to work at it. God blesses the work of our hands, but it is up to us to still put in the work. We went to Christian counselor. We also took an online communications course that the counselor recommended. Some of these courses ended in shouting matches – but we kept trying. We changed a lot of things in our normal day to day. One of the biggest changes we made was to change churches. This change has not only impacted my husband and I, but also our entire family. I know it may seem strange to say this, but this was a key thing for us.

While I had many friends at my old church, my husband did not really have any connections. He did not have godly men to confide in or to serve as accountability partners. As soon as we made the switch, and we were in a church that both taught the Word of God with boldness and had many men who embraced him and were so committed to helping him, everything changed. The changes in him were almost instant! Our new church was alive! As we worship in church, the crowd reminds me of a river – constantly moving and swaying. The church is like a river where healing rivers flow - and that is what happened for us here.

After attending for about two months or so, my husband gave his testimony in front of the whole church. He confessed what he did to an entire congregation and talked about how God had changed him. He talked about how grateful he was for his godly wife who prayed and fasted for him. I sat in the audience crying, barely able to contain my joy as I recorded him.

My pastor prayed for me and said that I would struggle to remember any of what had happened. And though I am not there yet, I know I am close – all glory goes to God. If you are in this same place, remember, He that began a good work, will be faithful to finish it (Philippians 1:6).

Pray This

Dear Heavenly Father,

Thank you so much for restoring my marriage. Thank you for restoring me. Thank you for everything you have already done.

Today, I declare, I have the mind of Christ[1]. It is renewed and transformed[2]. Thank you for my new life. Thank you for the wisdom and discernment[3] to recognize a thought that is not from you. I cast down any thought[4] trying to take root.

Fill me with your Holy Spirit and use me. I will keep moving forward and never backward[5].

In Jesus mighty name I pray,

Amen

THE VERSES REFERENCED

1. **1 Corinthians 2:16 (**NLT) For, "Who can know the LORD's thoughts? Who knows enough to teach him?"

But we understand these things, for we have the mind of Christ.

2. **Romans 12:2** (NIV) Do not conform to the pattern of this world, but be transformed by the renewing of your mind. Then you will be able to test and approve what God's will is—his good, pleasing, and perfect will.

3. **Proverbs 2:6** (NKJV) For the LORD gives wisdom; From His mouth *come* knowledge and understanding;

4. **2 Corinthians 10:5** (NIV) We demolish arguments and every pretension that sets itself up against the knowledge of God, and we take captive every thought to make it obedient to Christ.

5. **Philippians 3:13-14** (NIV) Brothers and sisters, I do not consider myself yet to have taken hold of it. But one thing I do: Forgetting what is behind and straining toward what is ahead, I press on toward the goal to win the prize for which God has called me heavenward in Christ Jesus.

SAY THIS

In the name of Jesus, I declare:

- I am enjoying my new season in life and the new thing God is doing in my life.
- My mind is fully renewed, fully transformed, and fully healed.

- My mind stays focused on the Lord, and He keeps me in perfect peace.
- My family is thriving and growing closer together every day.
- I am more than a conqueror in Christ.

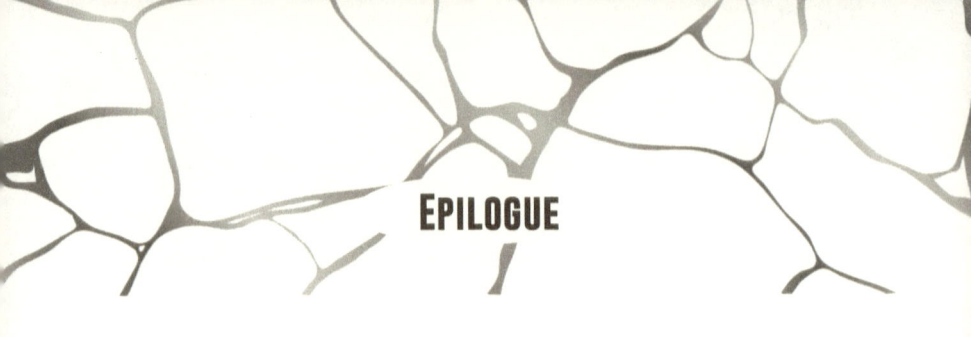

Life Now

This is the end of the book, but not the end of the story. There may be some chapters that you have to re-read, some prayers that you need to pray repeatedly. I did too. Do not stop repeating God's word and declaring what He says about you. Do it until it is so ingrained in you that no lie from the enemy can tell you otherwise. This is what I did and God restored my mind. He healed *me* first and then restored my marriage.

Our family life has resumed to a new normal. We are healed, fully restored and almost as if nothing had ever happened. Healthy boundaries have been set, but probably most importantly, the lukewarmness in our walk with the Lord and in regards to our marriage has changed.

If you are not there yet, please do not lose hope. Continue to **Pray Fierce**, for your marriage and be confident that He who began a good work in you **will** complete it (Philippians 1:6 NASB). Remember that **no good thing** will He withhold thing from those who walk uprightly (Psalms 84:11 NKJV).

I am sharing one last picture. It was taken during a cross-over service at our church at exactly 11:59pm on December 31, 2023 – one minute before the New Year. It is the first cross-over service we had ever been to as a couple and the first time I had worn a pink sequins blazer! We decided to take a selfie. It's not the best picture, but when I first looked at it, I smiled. I realized, I looked happy – we both did. And it's because I was – genuinely, genuinely happy.

The Salvation Prayer

I cannot end this book without including the Salvation Prayer. The Bible is full of promises for believers. People use the terms believer, saved, and Christian interchangeably, but what they all mean is that these people have decided to give their lives to Christ.

Being a Christian (or being a believer or being saved) is an act of surrender. We offer our past (what we've done), our present (all we are doing), and our future (all we will do) and give them all over to God, who designed us in the first place and who has a wonderful plan for our lives.

The Holy Bible reads, "for all have sinned and come short of the glory of God" and "for the wages of sin is death, but the gift of God is eternal life through Jesus Christ our Lord." Romans 10:9- 10 (NIV) also declares "If you declare with your mouth, "Jesus is Lord" and believe in your heart that God raised him from the dead, you will be saved. For it is with your heart that you believe and are justified, and it is with your mouth that you profess your faith and are saved."

If you are ready to take that step, say the following prayer out loud.

Pray This

Jesus,

Come into my heart. Forgive me of my sin. Wash me and cleanse me. Set me free.

Jesus, thank You that You died for me. I believe that You are risen from the dead, and that You are coming back again for me. Fill me with the Holy Spirit. Give me a passion for the lost, a hunger for the things of God, and a holy boldness to preach the gospel of Jesus Christ.

Amen.

That's it! You are saved! You are born again! And you are on your way to heaven because you have Jesus in your heart! Remember, never run away from God – run *to* Him because He loves you and has a wonderful plan for your life.

What's next? Tell someone! Learn! Find a local church.

www.ingramcontent.com/pod-product-compliance
Lightning Source LLC
Chambersburg PA
CBHW020333130626
46549CB00003B/1166